Contents

Outside

HOUGHTON MIFFLIN   BOSTON

Printed in China

ISBN-13: 978-0-618-93215-3
ISBN-10: 0-618-93215-1

1 2 3 4 5 6 7 8 9 SDP 15 14 13 12 11 10 09 08

Words to Know

cove   mole

hole   rose

home

beautiful

Beautiful or Not?

by Mary Lindeen

Beautiful is a nice word.

Here is a red rose.

Is a rose beautiful?

Here is a cove.

Is a cove beautiful?

Here is a big pine tree.
Is a pine tree beautiful?

Here is a mole.

Its home is in a hole.

Is a mole beautiful?

dunes   Luke

June   tube

even   beautiful

quiet

June's Home

by Mary Lindeen

illustrated by John Kurtz

June Mole likes her home.
It is up at Hope Cove.

June gets a tube from Luke.
A note is in it.
Luke gave June a kite kit!

June makes a fine big kite.
She even makes a rose on it.

June rides to the dunes.

The beautiful cove is quiet.

Up, up, up goes the kite!